A GUY'S GUIDE

Surviving School

Managing School
and Career Paths

ABDO
Publishing Company

A GUY'S GUIDE

Surviving School

Managing School and Career Paths

by J Chris Roselius

Content Consultant
Dr. Robyn J. A. Silverman
Child/Teen Development Expert and Success Coach
Powerful Words Character Development

Credits

Published by ABDO Publishing Company, 8000 West 78th Street, Edina, Minnesota 55439. Copyright © 2011 by Abdo Consulting Group, Inc. International copyrights reserved in all countries. No part of this book may be reproduced in any form without written permission from the publisher. The Essential Library™ is a trademark and logo of ABDO Publishing Company.

Printed in the United States of America,
North Mankato, Minnesota
062010
092010

Editor: Melissa Johnson
Copy Editor: Richard Reece
Interior Design and Production: Marie Tupy
Cover Design: Marie Tupy

Library of Congress Cataloging-in-Publication Data
Roselius, J Chris.
  Surviving school : managing school and career paths / J. Chris Roselius ; content consultant, Robyn J.A. Silverman.
    p. cm. — (Essential health, a guy's guide)
  Includes bibliographical references.
  ISBN 978-1-61613-544-7
  1. High school student orientation—United States—Juvenile literature. 2. High school boys—Vocational guidance—United States—Juvenile literature. 3. Boys—Education (Secondary)—United States—Juvenile literature. 4. Boys—Education (Middle school)—United States—Juvenile literature. I. Title.

  LB1620.6.R67 2011
  373.1821—dc22
                                                    2010017090

contents

Meet Dr. Robyn

Dr. Robyn Silverman truly enjoys spending time with young people. In fact, it's what she does best! As a child and teen development specialist, Dr. Robyn has devoted her career to helping guys just like you become all they can be—and possibly more than they ever imagined. Throughout this series, you'll read her expert advice on friends, girls, classmates, school, family, and everything in between.

A self-esteem and body image expert, Dr. Robyn takes a positive approach to life. She knows how tough it is to be a kid in today's world, and she's prepared with encouragement and guidance to help you become your very best and realize your goals.

Dr. Robyn helps young people share their wildest dreams and biggest problems. Her compassion, openness, and honesty make her trusted by many adolescents, and she considers it a gift to be able to interact with the young people whom she sees as the leaders of tomorrow. She created the Powerful Words Character Development system, a program taught all over the world in martial arts and other sports programs to help guys just like you become examples to others in their communities.

As a speaker, success coach, and award-winning author, Dr. Robyn's powerful messages have reached thousands of people. Her expert advice has been featured in *Prevention* magazine, *Parenting* magazine, *U.S. News and World Report*, and the *Washington Post*. She was an expert for *The Tyra Show*, *Fox News*, and NBC's *LXtv*. She has an online presence, too. You can follow her on Twitter, become a fan on Facebook, and read her blog on her Web site, www.DrRobynSilverman.com. When she isn't working, Dr. Robyn enjoys spending time with her family in New Jersey.

Dr. Robyn believes that young people are assets to be developed, not problems to be fixed. As she puts it, "Guys are so much more than the way the media paints them. They have so many things to offer. I'm ready to highlight how guys get it right and tips for the ways they can make their teen years the best years so far . . . I'd be grateful if you'd come along for the ride."

Take It from Me

Remember what elementary school was like? You worried about stuff like losing a tooth or who would hang out with you during recess. Now that you're older, problems are more complicated. The good news is that you also have better skills to tackle them. Maybe you want to get good grades, but you're worried it's not cool to do well in school. Maybe you're stressed from all the different activities you want to do. Maybe you deal with a learning disability or feel pressure to choose a career path. School can come with an assortment of anxieties and fears.

I went through a lot of that stuff when I was your age. I wanted to seem cool and act like school was no big deal, but I really cared about being a good student. I didn't have to deal with a learning disability, but I had a friend who did and saw how much he struggled at times. I remember the first time I had to speak for several minutes in front of a class. I was so nervous I could barely stand up.

You probably already know how to face a lot of difficult situations. Sometimes you'll be able to get through them pretty easily. Other times you're going to fall down at first, only to get up and try again. Still other times, you might fail completely or need extra help.

That's okay. Learning how to get through challenges will help you grow as a person.

That's all fine to hear, but does knowing that help you when you're in the middle of a tough situation? Not really. It's frustrating when people say, "Oh, don't worry. It's not the end of the world." I get that. Sometimes you need to learn about other guys' situations and what they've done. I hope the stories in this book will help.

Don't stress!

Chris

1

The Poser

Even if you took away homework, school would still be a challenge. School cliques and groups—including your own—can be stressful. Maybe your school has a lot of groups. But there are probably two main ones—the cool kids and the not-cool kids.

The pressure to be cool and popular is intense, especially for guys. Even guys with a lot of friends may think they don't have enough of the "right" friends. Some guys will do whatever they can to be cool, from acting or dressing differently to playing the right sport. To make things worse, guys are not supposed to care about being cool. For guys, trying to be cool is uncool.

Some guys have no problem not being popular. They don't worry about what others think or say about them. But other guys will try anything to be popular. Tony is a guy like that.

Tony's Story

Tony and Rob had been friends since second grade. They used to be best friends, but since middle school started they hadn't been hanging out that much. It was like they didn't have as much in common as they used to. For one thing, Tony was into school. He studied hard and usually got all As.

> To make things worse, guys are not supposed to care about being cool. For guys, trying to be cool is uncool.

He was also into chess. Rob, on the other hand, was happy with Bs and Cs, or at least he pretended to be. And Rob was really good at soccer.

"Seriously," Rob said to Tony one day after school. "You're becoming a total nerd. You're bad for my image, man." Rob pretended he was joking, but Tony knew he really wasn't. The last three times Tony had invited Rob to hang out, Rob had been too busy.

"Sorry, dude," Rob had said when Tony had invited him over to play Wii, "I'm going somewhere with Isaac this afternoon." The next time Rob had been busy with Rashid, then Michelle, Lisa, and Jake, who everyone knew was the best football player in the school.

Tony only had two other friends—Mark and Jasper from chess club. Why was it so easy for Rob to make friends? Tony wondered. He decided that Rob had everything that mattered—good looks, good clothes, and athletic ability. Some people made fun of Tony because he got good grades, but no one ever teased Rob for failing to do well in class.

Think About It

- What happened between you and your elementary school friends when you entered middle school? Did those friendships change?

- Do you feel pressure to fit into a group?

- Are grades important at your school? Is being athletic or having cool clothes more important?

- Do people at your school make fun of kids who make good grades? If so, why do you think that happens?

Tony had never felt like an outsider before. When he was younger, he'd been happy with the friends he had. He liked making his parents proud with his good grades. But something was different now. It bugged him that he wasn't invited to parties like Rob. He wanted to hang out with Rob again—and Rob's popular friends, too.

Tony thought about what he had to do. He was actually pretty athletic, but he just wasn't very interested in sports. The only real difference between Rob and Tony was their grades. Tony decided he needed to change that.

Think About It

• Why do you think Tony started to worry about not being cool once he got to middle school? Did you, or someone you know, ever feel like Tony?

• Have you ever felt like you needed to be cooler? What did you do about it?

On purpose, Tony stopped doing some homework. When he got a bad grade on a test, he put the paper right out on his desk, hoping Rob would see. "Mr. Carlson's high if he thinks I care," he said loudly after class. But Rob and his friends didn't seem to notice.

"What's with you, Tony?" Jasper asked him. Tony just shrugged. That afternoon he skipped chess club. Instead he went to the mall and spent all his savings to buy clothes he thought Rob and the cool kids would wear.

Tony thought he would show up, do something insanely cool, and become the most popular guy in school.

Tony's teachers noticed the sudden dip in his grades. They started to wonder if he was having problems at home. Jasper and Mark were worried, too. "Tony, what's going on?" they asked. But he told them to leave him alone.

"Hey, Rob, what's up?" he called out to his former friend one day on the way to gym. "You goin'

to Jake's party tonight?" But Rob barely even turned around to answer him. "Yeah—don't tell me you are."

But Tony knew he had to go to the party even though he wasn't invited. He felt like he had to take a chance. In movies, the cool group always realized the nerd was all right when he made some kind of big gesture, like suddenly becoming the life of the party. Tony thought he would show up, do something insanely cool, and become the most popular guy in school.

Tony was so nervous, though. He thought
of bailing on his plan a thousand times. But that
night, he showed up at the party anyway. He walked
in behind a group of kids he recognized, but once

inside, he regretted his move. He just stood in a corner with his arms crossed against his chest.

He saw Rob standing with a group of guys and nodded his head at him. Rob gave him a thumbs-up. Then he turned back to his friends. "What a poser," he said, and they all cracked up.

Rob gave him a thumbs-up. Then he turned back to his friends. "What a poser," he said, and they all cracked up.

Tony had to get out of there. He stumbled for the door. He heard more laughter as he ran down the front steps and toward home.

Think About It

- Have you ever known a person trying to "fit in" like Tony? How did you treat him?

- Why do you think Rob and his friends laughed at Tony?

- What could Tony have done instead of running out of the party?

Wanting to be popular is totally normal. Friends are important to you and their opinions matter. You want to become more independent, and you're looking for acceptance outside of your family. You often tend to gravitate toward guys who share your interests. At the same time, you want to belong to the right group.

It can hurt pretty bad to feel like an outsider. You might start doing things you never thought you would. Most of the time, the desire to fit in affects the superficial areas of a guy's life, like what clothes he wears, the music he listens to, or the way he talks. They may be no big deal. It's more serious, though, if you act like Tony, letting your grades slip and turning your back on the friends you already have. Acting like that could produce some pretty serious consequences. And they probably won't get you what you want, either. As Tony's story shows, kids are pretty harsh on guys they think are "posers." When you pretend to be someone you're not, people will like you only for who you are pretending to be. When you are true to yourself, people will like you for who you really are.

Work It Out

1. The key to being truly cool is being yourself. People can see right through someone who is fake or trying too hard.

2. Try getting involved with some groups outside of school. You might make some new friends who share your interests.

3. Form your own group based on common interests—video games, music, chess, or anything you like. Believe it or not, a lot of so-called popular kids would secretly love to join you.

The Last Word from Chris

Wanting to fit in is natural for any guy. But remember, you shouldn't change who you are to try to be cool. If you like working hard to get good grades, if you wear clothes no one else is wearing, or if you listen to music others consider weird, then do that. Don't try to change who you are just to fit in with a certain crowd. Those people aren't going to be your real friends anyway. There are a lot of guys just like you who share your interests. Those are the people who will matter to you most in the long run.

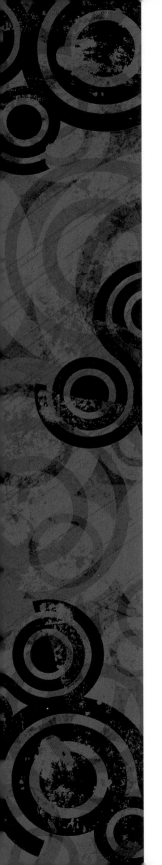

2
The Overachiever

veryone knows the overachiever. He plays numerous sports. He also does after-school activities, such as theater or debate. And he still has time to do well in class. A guy like that makes it look easy. For some, maybe it is easy. But for a lot of guys, balancing so many things is difficult.

Some guys join a ton of groups because they think it will make them popular. Or they want to please someone, maybe a teacher or their parents. Some guys have many interests or can't decide what they want to do, so they try to do everything.

By doing too many things, it becomes difficult to focus on the one or two things that matter most to you. You may get stressed out, and that can lead to lack of sleep or concentration problems. Hudson got mixed up in too many activities and ended up facing his own set of issues.

Hudson's Story

The bell rang. It was 3:00, finally. Hudson shoved his books into his backpack and raced down the hall.

"Hey, Hudson, wait up!" yelled Craig.

"Sorry, Craig, not now," Hudson called back without slowing down. He had to get to the student council meeting early. That way, maybe

> By doing too many things, it becomes difficult to focus on the one or two things that matter most to you.

he'd have a few minutes to start his math homework. Mr. Monroe had assigned the problems last week to give the students "plenty of time." But Hudson hadn't had a chance to do even one yet. He had always been a good student, especially in math, but lately he just didn't have the time. Football practice took up most afternoons. Monday was yearbook. Tuesday he had a piano recital. (Hudson felt embarrassed remembering his performance. He *had* to figure out a way to let his mom know he wanted to quit.) Now today, Wednesday, was student council.

Hudson picked up his pace. Suddenly he felt a shove and heard things clattering on the floor.

"Hey, watch it!" someone said.

Hudson looked down. "Oh, sorry, Megan,"
Hudson said. He bent down to help his friend pick
up her stuff.

"It's okay." Megan flashed Hudson one of her
bright smiles. Like most everybody in their class,

Megan really liked Hudson. What wasn't there to like? He was cute, smart, athletic, and totally together. In fact, Megan was the one who suggested he run for student council. And he had beaten the other guy by a landslide.

"See ya, Megan." Hudson ran off to the meeting. Today's topic was new water fountains, and he owed it to the kids who voted for him to be there.

Think About It

- why do you think Hudson wanted to be involved in so many activities?

- why do you think Hudson is taking piano lessons?

- Have you ever been involved with activities that conflicted with each other? what did you do?

In September, Hudson had been psyched to get back to school and get busy. After summer vacation, he was ready for a change of pace. By October, though, he had something going on almost every day after school. And school was getting harder, too. The science fair was coming up, and Hudson hadn't even thought of a good topic for his project.

Just thinking about everything he had to do made Hudson's heart beat faster. At night sometimes, when he was trying to fall asleep, his mind would race. He'd worry about getting everything done, so he'd get out of bed to do homework or study for a test, but he was too tired to concentrate. The next morning, he was wiped out. Sometimes he dreaded going to a yearbook or student council meeting.

Hudson managed to finish his algebra homework by staying up late Wednesday night. But when he walked into history on Thursday morning, he was in for a rude surprise.

"Okay, everyone. Please take your seats right now," Mrs. Jaffrey was calling out when he walked into the room that day.

Test! Hudson had totally forgotten! He guessed at half the questions and left several blank.

He had remembered about the quiz on *To Kill a Mockingbird* in English later in the day. He'd even skimmed through the book. But he couldn't seem to remember anything he'd read.

That afternoon was football practice. Usually, Hudson was one of the fastest players on defense, but today he was dragging.

"Move it, Hudson!" Coach Travis yelled.

"Leave me alone," Hudson muttered under his breath.

"You have something to say?" Coach asked.

"No, Coach," Hudson said, catching up with the others. It had already been a terrible day. He didn't need to finish it off with 20 extra push-ups.

Think About It

- Why is Hudson having trouble remembering things?

- Have you ever been so overscheduled that you start to resent the things you are doing? When? How did you handle the situation?

- How could Hudson have handled football practice differently?

"Hudson . . . honey?"

Hudson opened his eyes. His mom was sitting on the edge of his bed. Light was streaming through the blinds. Hudson shot up. It was 8:30!

"I'm late! Why did you let me sleep so late?" he yelled at his mother.

"You're not going to school today," Hudson's mom said. "You're exhausted, and I'm exhausted seeing what's happening to you. Both of us are having a mental health day."

That day, Hudson and his mom went for a bike ride. They ate sandwiches on the patio. In the afternoon, they read. Hudson tried *To Kill a Mockingbird* again. For the first time in weeks, he was able to relax and really get into a book. It was amazing how much he'd missed before!

Hudson opened his eyes. His mom was sitting on the edge of his bed. Light was streaming through the blinds. Hudson shot up. It was 8:30!

That night, Hudson and his parents had a talk.

"We're proud of you for being such a talented, responsible person," his dad said. "But things are getting ridiculous. Mrs. Jaffrey says you're struggling in history, and Coach Travis tells me that you don't seem to be having as much fun in football."

"You need to cut out some of your activities," Hudson's mom said.

"How can I?" Hudson said. "Everybody's counting on me . . . even you guys."

Hudson's mom smiled a little. "I know you hate piano," she said. "And it's okay with me if you want to take a break from that for a while."

Hudson smiled back. Already it felt like a weight had lifted from his shoulders.

That night, Hudson made a list of all his responsibilities: school, football, piano, yearbook, and student council. Then he added things that he'd like to do but didn't have time for: hanging out with friends, reading, learning to play the drums. Then he numbered his list, with 1 being the most important (school, obviously) and 8 the least (piano). He agreed to focus only on the top three items: school, football, and drums. This left him with plenty of free time for just hanging out with his friends, too.

Hudson smiled back. Already it felt like a weight had lifted from his shoulders.

It wasn't easy, but the next day he told the other group members that he was dropping student council and the yearbook. They actually understood a lot better than he thought they would.

"I could never figure out how you did it all, anyway," Megan said. "I'm glad to see that you're human like the rest of us."

Think About It

- How does Hudson walk the line between balancing his own wishes against the wishes of others? Does he stay true to himself?

- Have your parents ever pressured you to take up an activity you didn't want to do? How did it turn out?

- Have you been forced to choose between doing one activity over another? How did you make the decision?

Think about why a guy might get into too many activities. Perhaps he wants to please his parents and teachers, or his friends are pressuring him. A guy could end up seriously stressed out trying to make other people happy. Hudson is that type of guy. He needed to identify his true interests and then focus on them.

But what if you join things because all the choices sound so good? If you're like that, you could try one thing at a time. Commit to activities that you can handle. Instead of signing up for a yearlong activity like student council, for example, volunteer for a smaller project, such as a week of community cleanup. Then, when it's over, you can think about what you want to do next.

A big part of not getting in too deep is being honest about who you are. Are you the kind of person who needs a lot of sleep? Do you like a lot of downtime? How do your parents feel? Be careful not to spread yourself too thin. In that situation, you can't give anything your all.

And don't forget, the most important things are school and your health. Those come first, no matter what.

Work It Out

1. Before choosing an activity, make sure you can commit to it. How much time does It take each week? How long does it last? What other commitments do you have?

2. Make sure you rank your activities by importance. Don't let one activity dominate your time, or take you away from an activity you enjoy more.

3. If you start to feel overwhelmed, talk to your parents or another adult for guidance.

4. Try not to let extracurricular activities become more important than your schoolwork.

The Last Word from Chris

It's weird, isn't it? Sometimes by doing too much you end up with too little. You might need to focus more to succeed. Sometimes, as it was with Hudson, dropping out is the answer. That's why it's important to be careful about what you take on in the first place. One thing at a time is the secret to success for a natural-born overachiever.

3
Making Progress

Higher expectations, body stuff, girls, fitting in: there are so many reasons this time in your life is tough. But for kids with learning disabilities, it's even harder.

Lots of very smart guys have learning disabilities. But for some reason, usually having to do with their brain chemistry, they have trouble learning in certain areas. In the United States, about one in five kids has a learning disability.

You've probably heard of dyslexia. It's a learning disorder that mostly affects a person's ability to learn to read and spell. It can make a guy feel really bad about himself. But many people who suffer from dyslexia are smart, even

geniuses, in their areas of interest. They include inventor Thomas Edison, actor Tom Cruise, and basketball legend Magic Johnson.

Ike has dyslexia. It makes for rough going sometimes, but he finds a way to deal with the challenge.

Ike's Story

Three weeks until summer vacation—Ike could *not* wait. Sure, all guys love the end of the year, but things were different for Ike. He just could not take school anymore.

Things hadn't been so bad in elementary school. Ike enjoyed math. He loved art and was awesome at gym. Because of his dyslexia, he did

Lots of very smart guys have learning disabilities. But for some reason, usually having to do with their brain chemistry, they have trouble learning in certain areas.

need extra help with reading, but he got by, and his teachers were proud of him. But now, it seemed like *everything* was about reading. Every day, he had pages of reading for homework. He'd crack open his books around 6:00 p.m. By 8:30, he'd gotten less than halfway through what he needed to do.

"Focus on your progress," Mr. Isaacson, Ike's reading teacher, advised. "And you *are* making progress, Ike."

Maybe. But not fast enough, and not like the other kids. That was the other thing about Ike's "problem." He'd heard Derrik Morril call him "stupid" in the halls yesterday—and at least two other kids had laughed about it.

Ike could not wait for summer. In his mind, "summer" meant "alone."

Think About It

- Do you or anyone else you know have dyslexia or another learning disability? How do you or that other person handle it?

- Have you ever made fun of someone who has a learning disability? If so, how did you feel about it afterward?

- Once in a while, everybody feels like they just want to be left alone. when this happens to you, what are the reasons? How do you handle the problem?

Ike wanted to be away from everyone, except for maybe Dan, his best friend. Although Dan lived next door, he went to a different school from Ike. He knew Ike for who he was—not for his achievement in school. Maybe that's why it was so easy for Dan to recognize that Ike was actually very smart.

"You're like a genius in art," Dan had told Ike after Ike showed him a sculpture he'd made from a fallen branch in his yard. Dan was good at art, too. He made amazing black-and-white designs.

When Ike came home from school one day, Dan came running up to him.

"Check this out!" he said. Dan was holding something in his hand. It was a flyer about a summer art camp downtown at the Art Institute. "I'm going," he said, "and my mom said she'd talk to your parents about it."

Ike leafed through the brochure. One photo showed a bunch of kids sitting at easels with a teacher in the front of the room. "I don't know, Danny," Ike said. The whole thing sounded a lot like school. What if some freaky teacher made them take turns reading aloud about some artist? What if it turned out he wasn't as good as he thought? Then he'd be bad at reading *and* art.

Think About It

- Have you ever had a problem that kept you from doing something new?

- what common activities do you share with your friends? Have you ever tried to help a friend do more with his or her talent?

Ike's parents encouraged him to do the summer camp. He was still nervous, but they convinced him to go. On the first day, Ike realized right away that he'd made the right decision. The counselors were awesome, and the other kids were cool, too. Everyone admired his artwork, and his dyslexia didn't matter to anyone. He learned some new techniques, too, like oil painting and mixed media.

The whole thing sounded a lot like school. What if some freaky teacher made them take turns reading aloud about some artist?

Ike's parents also hired a tutor and made him practice reading one hour every day. Ike got to read

whatever he wanted. One thing he found was a biography of the famous artist Pablo Picasso. He read that Picasso probably had dyslexia, just like him. That blew Ike's mind.

At the end of summer, Ike's mother gave him a reward for how hard he'd worked on both his reading and his art—she said that he could paint his bedroom any way he wanted. She even bought the materials Ike needed for the project he had in mind. In addition to reading every day, he painted.

Ike's mother also met with Mr. Isaacson about adjusting Ike's IEP, or Individual Education Plan. "I don't want you struggling with your homework the way you were last year," she explained to Ike. Mr. Isaacson agreed that Ike's teachers needed to come up with some new strategies for helping Ike.

When school started again in the fall, Ike wasn't exactly thrilled, but at least he wasn't dreading it.

"Ike, I see you've made a lot of progress over the summer," Mr. Isaacson said when he and Ike met for reading help. Ike smiled. It was true.

Think About It

- What's in store for Ike? Do you think he's in better shape to face his schoolwork? Why?

- Is there something outside of school that you're really good at, the way Ike is with art? How do you fit it in? Does it help you do better at school?

A lot of people don't understand dyslexia and other learning disorders. For one thing, just because a guy has dyslexia or a learning disorder does not mean he is not intelligent. However, dyslexia is not something that a guy can outgrow. Guys with dyslexia can make a lot of progress. However, they must find alternative ways to learn so that they can successfully cope with the disability throughout their lives. They still may struggle, but these strategies can make it easier for them to become whatever they want to be.

Ike is luckier than some other guys. When he was just learning to read, a professional identified his dyslexia. Identifying dyslexia is hard because many teachers are not trained to spot it, especially since reading problems can stem from other factors. So unlike other kids, Ike is not struggling alone. His parents and teachers know how to help him.

Unfortunately, dyslexia can really hurt a guy's self-esteem, especially when it's combined with mean remarks like "stupid" or "lazy" from people who don't understand. One of the best ways for a guy to fight low self-esteem is to find something he's good at and pursue it. That's what Ike did with art. Ike's problems are not solved, but he can cope.

Work It Out

1. If you are suffering from dyslexia, remember that you are not alone. A lot of successful people suffer from dyslexia, such as actor Whoopi Goldberg and even writers like John Grisham and John Irving.

2. Make sure you become involved in activities that you love and at which you can excel. This will give you self-confidence that will carry over to all areas of your life.

3. If you are struggling in school, talk to your parents. They can find services or interventions to help you.

The Last Word from Chris

Believe it or not, dyslexia is not all bad. Scientific research shows that the same biological factors that cause dyslexia in a guy may also make him more creative. Maybe that's why so many people with dyslexia have gone on to become leaders in arts, business, and science. But it's hard to do anything if you don't like yourself. To me, that seems like the biggest problem. So, if you have dyslexia, work hard at reading, find something that you're good at, and keep your chin up.

4

Testing the Future

In an increasingly competitive world, many people believe it can never be too early to start thinking about your career. A lot of that has to do with the high cost of college. Changing your major multiple times can increase the years you spend in college. And that could cost thousands of extra dollars.

You can even take aptitude tests to see what fields would likely be the best fit for you. Some parents use these tests to try to guide their child into a career. These parents believe they are doing what is right for their child. But aptitude tests are just guides. The result of a test should not be the only factor in your career choice. Plus, at this age, you

have a lot of the world to experience before deciding what you want to do as an adult. Juan's parents tried pushing him down a particular career path. Here is his story.

At this age, you have a lot of the world to experience before deciding what you want to do as an adult.

Juan's Story

Juan grew up wanting to be a lawyer, just like his dad. But one day, Juan decided he would rather be a firefighter. Then he watched a movie about space travel and decided he wanted to be an astronaut. Of course, at the time he was only eight years old. As Juan grew older, he continued to imagine himself in all kinds of possible careers. He loved that the future was filled with so many exciting possibilities.

By middle school, Juan's teachers and parents realized he was really good at math. He understood the concepts behind math and was able to solve most problems pretty quickly. On tests in school and standardized tests, he always earned or came close to earning the top score.

But Juan had a ton of other interests as well. He liked history and writing, and even though he was really good in math, it wasn't one of his favorite subjects in school. He also loved to play soccer. It didn't matter that he wasn't the best player. His teammates were some of his best friends, and he loved being part of a team.

Think About It

- Why do you think Juan had so many interests?

- If Juan was so good in math, why do you think it wasn't his favorite subject?

- Is your favorite subject the one you're best in?

Juan's parents had always encouraged him to prepare for the next step in life. They taught him to read when he was very young so he'd be ready for kindergarten. When he finished elementary school, they put him in summer school to do extra prep work for middle school. Now that Juan was in middle school, they took Juan to a career-counseling service. They wanted Juan to know in advance what classes he should take in high school to prepare for his future. The counselor there would test his skills and help determine what careers he might be good at as an adult.

"Well, Juan," began the counselor. "The tests show that your strongest aptitude is math. There are many great careers that would let you use this skill. Engineer, physicist, architect. Finance, computer programming. Really, the sky's the limit."

The counselor gave Juan a bunch of brochures and recommended that he take classes such as calculus and physics in high school. Juan felt overwhelmed by all the information. The classes sounded hard, too. He worried that he wouldn't be up to the challenge.

Think About It

- Have you ever taken a career or aptitude test? Did the results match what you think your strengths are?

- Do you know what profession you want to be in when you grow up? If so, how do you know it will be the right career for you?

That night after dinner, Juan and his parents sat down to discuss the career test results.

"Juan, you are so good at math. I think you should focus on that and get a head start for college and your career," Juan's dad said.

"College costs so much, dear," added Juan's mom. "We'd hate to see you struggle there and maybe take extra time to graduate. More prep work now will make college so much easier."

"We're putting you in extra classes on Saturdays to help you take calculus sooner when you get to high school," explained Juan's dad.

"But I have games on Saturdays," Juan said. "I don't know if I want to miss that much playing time."

His dad shrugged a bit. "You'll have to leave the soccer team because you won't be able to make weekend games."

Juan looked at both his parents' faces. He could see that they loved him, and they really believed that the classes would be best for him. He agreed to quit sports and focus on math and science. *Besides,* he thought, *I was never going to be a pro soccer player anyway. This is better for my future.*

Think About It

- why did Juan's parents think he should start to focus on math and science classes?

- what do you think about Juan's parents' decision to have Juan quit soccer? what would you do if you were Juan?

Juan started the extra classes. At first, he learned many new things. Soon, he was studying trigonometry, something that most students don't learn until a year or two into high school. After a few weeks, though, his progress began to slow.

Every day was the same thing—take this math class, go to that science class. He didn't even get the weekend off, since the extra classes plus homework took all his free time.

It didn't take long for him to start dreading school. He started doodling and daydreaming during

class, things he had never done before. He missed playing soccer more than he thought he would, too.

When Juan came home from school, he started going straight to his room. He felt like he had to study all the time. If he was hiding in his room, his parents couldn't tell when he was just staring off into space.

When Juan got a C on his next chapter test, he knew his grades were going to be in trouble at

It didn't take long for him to start dreading school. He started doodling and daydreaming during class, things he had never done before.

the end of the quarter. He was mad at himself—he knew he could do better than that. But it was so hard to concentrate and study because he was so burned out from all the extra work. *If only I could just play soccer again*, he thought. *I just need a break!*

Juan knew he'd be in big trouble if he brought home bad grades. Steeling himself, he decided to talk to his parents about quitting the Saturday math classes. One evening before dinner, he sat down with his parents and told them everything.

"I want to make you proud of me," Juan explained. "But I need a break from all these classes. I want to play soccer. And I miss my friends."

Juan was astonished to see his parents nodding sympathetically.

"Juan, it's okay. We wanted you to get a head start," explained his mom. "But we don't want you to end up hating math, either. You can quit the extra classes and join soccer again if you work to bring your grades back up in school."

Juan was surprised—and grateful. He thought he'd be in big trouble. But instead, it seemed as though his parents understood after all.

Think About It

- why do you think Juan's grades started to slip and his mood changed so much?

- Have you ever been forced to take classes you didn't enjoy? How did you handle the situation?

- Have you ever been afraid to tell your parents something because you thought what you had to say would disappoint them?

The pressure to find the right job is tremendous today. Parents want their children to be fully prepared. In order to get ahead, some parents believe their children need to start focusing on a career early.

Some teenagers already have a strong idea of what they want to do. So focusing on certain classes is no problem for them. But many others have no idea what they want to be when they grow up. They are still trying to figure out who they really are. Even adults question their career choice from time to time. Many people work in one career for years only to start doing something completely different later in life.

You might think it would be nice to know what you want to do early in your life. But choosing a career path is complicated and shouldn't be decided quickly. Give yourself time to learn as much as possible about potential careers before choosing your path. Going to a counselor may be helpful, but your counselor can't decide what's best for you.

In preparing for the future, don't overschedule yourself. You need a break sometimes, too!

Work It Out

1. If people are trying to steer you toward a certain profession that you aren't interested in, calmly tell them how you feel. Show them what you would really be good at instead, or just tell them you haven't decided.

2. When you think about your future, consider multiple options. If your first choice doesn't work out, it's always good to have backup plans.

3. Ask questions. Learning more about a career can help you prepare for it and decide if you're truly interested in it.

The Last Word from Chris

There will always be people trying to give you career advice—your family, your friends, your teachers, your counselors. They just want to help you. But in the end, you have to choose a career that is right for you. If you are being pushed to go into a certain field that you really aren't interested in, don't be afraid to speak up. A job is something you will be doing five days a week, so you want to do everything you can to make sure you are happy with it.

5
Anxiety Test

Few people enjoy taking standardized tests. These tests measure how well you're doing in certain subjects compared to your entire state or even the country! Some students have to pass the test to move on to the next grade. With all that pressure, who wouldn't be nervous? For some guys, however, test anxiety is almost too much to handle. In fact, it can be crippling.

You can prepare for the test for weeks and be sure you know everything. But some guys suffer from test anxiety. As the test nears, nervousness can make their minds go blank. Physical changes might happen as well—like a

fast heartbeat, dizziness, an upset stomach, nausea. If this happens to you, all you want is to get out of that room and away from the test. Terrell was a good student, but he always struggled at taking standardized tests. Can he handle his anxiety?

Terrell's Story

"Michael, Jenny, Anna, Terrell . . ." Mrs. Guest passed back their history reports. Terrell glanced at his paper—a 96 percent. Terrell was pleased. He studied hard in all his classes and got mostly As with some Bs. He always

For some guys, however, test anxiety is almost too much to handle. In fact, it can be crippling.

did well when he had a report to do, and he usually got through regular tests all right. But bigger exams were a different matter.

"Good job, class," Mrs. Guest continued. "I think you will all be ready next month for the history section in the state exams. Remember, you have to pass in order to move up to the next grade."

A sweat broke out on Terrell's forehead. Even thinking about the state exams made his hands shake and his heart beat faster. The high stakes and high pressure of the big standardized tests completely freaked Terrell out every time. He shoved the report in his backpack. The A didn't seem so great now. *What's the point of good grades*, thought Terrell, *if I fail the big exam?*

Terrell knew that if he failed, he would have to take—and pass—the test during the summer, or else he would repeat eighth grade. Terrell was terrified of that, especially since his friends didn't know he struggled so much with standardized tests.

After class, his buddy Aiden asked if Terrell wanted to study with some other people, maybe making it easier for them to prepare. "Nah, that's okay," said Terrell. "I'll just study by myself. Thanks for the offer."

Think About It

- why do you think Terrell didn't want to study with Aiden?

- Are you afraid to take standardized tests? If so, how do you deal with your fear?

- Do you feel more pressure when you take a standardized test compared to a normal test in school?

Starting two weeks before the big test, Aiden and his other friends met each day after school and went over possible test material. They asked their teachers what topics would likely be on the test and learned it would cover math, science, reading comprehension, and history. They worked on a different subject every day.

Meanwhile, Terrell watched television after school or played video games. He was so nervous about the test that he didn't even want to think about it. With one week left before the test, Terrell started to study. He had been trying so hard to ignore the test that he didn't really know what he needed to concentrate on. He looked over math problems for a few minutes every day and then switched to science for a few more minutes, then reading and history, doing a little of every topic every day.

Think About It

- whose approach to studying for the big test was better, Aiden's or Terrell's? Do you study more like Aiden or more like Terrell?

- why do you think Terrell put off studying for the test?

One day before the test, Terrell was already getting nervous, nearly to the point of feeling sick. Walking home with Aiden, he asked his friend how he felt about the test.

"I'm feeling pretty good," Aiden answered with a smile. "We've been studying, and I think I'm ready. I'm gonna look at a couple of things tonight and then go to bed early."

Terrell was amazed at how calm Aiden seemed to be! How could he be ready? Terrell didn't think he was ready at all. He decided he needed to stay in his

room and study everything he had gone over once again.

When Terrell got home, he ran straight upstairs to his room. His mom knocked on the door and asked him to come down to dinner. "I can't, Mom," he called through the door. "I have to study!" He didn't mention that he was also too nervous to eat.

He studied for hours, skimming quickly through all his notes and paging through each textbook. It was past midnight when he finally went to bed. He went to bed, but not to sleep—he kept imagining all the things that could go wrong at the test. He had a lot of trouble falling asleep.

At 7:00 a.m., the alarm started to beep. Terrell woke with a start—he'd been dreaming that he showed up for the exam in his underwear, and then failed because he didn't have a No. 2 pencil.

Then, when he got his test, everything went blank! He couldn't remember anything he studied, even the material from the night before.

Terrell felt horrible. He was really sleepy, and he had a headache. When he got to school to take the test, he started to feel sick. Sweat started to form on his forehead. Then, when he got his test, everything went blank! He couldn't remember anything he studied, even the material from the night before. He glanced over at Aiden, who seemed to be answering the questions with ease.

More and more, Terrell panicked. *Stupid!* he thought. *Why don't you know this!* He was able to answer a few questions, but when he looked at his watch, he saw that the time limit was nearly up. He quickly answered the remaining questions, but many

of his answers were guesses. When the test was over, Terrell knew he hadn't done well.

A couple of weeks later, he got his test score back. He failed! He would now have to take the test again during the summer. Worse, he would have to go through the process one more time.

Think About It

- Have you ever been nervous before taking a standardized test? Did it affect you during the test?

- What would you tell Terrell to do to prepare for retaking the test?

Taking a standardized test can be very nerve-wracking. Being nervous is natural. Some guys, however, suffer from severe test anxiety. Once you start to experience these symptoms, they can snowball, even affecting how well you prepare for the test. Terrell was a good student, but he didn't know how to control his anxiety. If you know you get too anxious to take exams well, seek help. There is no shame in suffering from test anxiety. Your parents, a teacher, or a counselor can guide you in overcoming your fear.

Research shows that an estimated 20 to 30 percent of students feel the effects of test anxiety. Responses vary from slight fear all the way to outright panic. It's not about their ability. It's about the test situation. But anxiety affects their test performance.

Terrell worried about the test before he even took it. Instead of being confident that he was going to pass, he was scared he was going to fail. You can't allow fear to be in the driver's seat. If you can't remember an answer, come back to it later. Being well prepared and confident about your success often leads to a better performance.

Work It Out

1. If you suffer from test anxiety, talk to an adult about it. Don't keep it a secret because it may become more serious.

2. Take a practice test. This will allow you to become more familiar with the test and give you more confidence.

3. Give yourself plenty of time to learn the material. Cramming is not an effective way to study.

4. Learn relaxation skills, such as taking deep breaths or imagining yourself being successful.

5. Tests are only one measurement. They do not predict your future success. Work hard and focus on your improvements.

The Last Word from Chris

Suffering from test anxiety can be frustrating. You know that you know the material—you just have trouble showing it during a high-pressure test. Sure, the stakes may be high—but don't let a standardized test defeat you before you have even taken it. Preparation is your best weapon.

6

Mr. Disorganized

Life at your age has a ton of changes. In addition to higher expectations, there's a lot of new stuff to keep track of. You switch classes for six or seven subjects now, not just art or music or gym. You have to make it to each room on time, maybe swinging by your locker to make sure you have all the right stuff. Then, each teacher does things a little differently. You have all kinds of homework due at various times. Maybe for the first time in your life, you can't just wing it. You *have* to be organized.

But how? Being organized at home and school is something you have to learn, just like most things. Kenny

learned the hard way how important it is to be organized.

Kenny's Story

"You can never find anything in this mess!" Kenny's mom said. Kenny felt like she was always walking into his room saying that.

Kenny looked around his room. "I'm in the middle of a lot of stuff," he explained to his mother. The floor was strewn with clothes, which were under papers, which were under a pile of wires he needed for some electronics thing he was supposed to be *Maybe for the first time in your life, you can't just wing it.* doing with his dad. . . . Kenny noticed that his iPod was sticking out of one of his sneakers.

"I've been looking for that!" he said, grabbing his music player.

"You'd find a lot of things you needed if you organized your room," his mom said. "Not to mention how much time you'd save in the morning."

It was true. Almost every morning, Kenny was rummaging through his room looking for something he needed—a shoe, his phone, math homework. He usually found what he was looking for—eventually. Several times he nearly missed the bus, though.

Kenny's locker at school was just as bad as his room. Even other kids laughed about it. Sometimes, Kenny would open it up, and books and papers would come spilling down in an avalanche. More than once, Kenny had been late to class because he was looking for something.

Think About It

- Do your parents tell you to clean your room a lot? Why do you think they're saying that?

- Have you been late to school because you were looking for something you'd misplaced?

- What does your locker look like at school? Do you try to keep it organized?

Kenny's teachers thought he was lazy and just didn't apply himself. But that wasn't the case. Kenny just didn't understand what the big deal was about

being neat. He'd always been this way, and he'd managed just fine. Besides, cleaning was *such* a chore.

After school, all Kenny wanted to do was put on his earphones and head home. One day, he was quickly shoving things into his backpack while listening to some music. He headed out, not noticing that he was missing a few things.

That night, he couldn't find his notes about what problems he was supposed to do for algebra the next day. He had to call his friend Mike to ask him. Then he couldn't find the copy of *Romeo and Juliet* he was supposed to be reading. His dad had to go dig out his old copy from the basement. By the time his dad found what Kenny needed, it was almost 9:30 p.m. Kenny tried to catch up on act II, but he was so tired. He could barely understand what was going on.

"Kenny," his dad said. "This is getting out of hand. You have to be more responsible." But then his dad helped him, the way he always did. "Let's read the play together. I'll tell you what's going on," he said, and Kenny handed over the book.

Think About It

- why did kenny's dad help him with reading Romeo and Juliet? was he right to do that? what would your parents have done?

- Do you think getting organized is a chore?

In February, Kenny had to start on a science report. It would count for 25 percent of his grade in that class. Kenny's topic was about pesticides and algae. It required research and a lot of writing, as well as graphs, charts, and photos.

Kenny was assigned the project one month before it was due. But when he got back to his locker, Mackenzie was waiting for him. "I've got something so awesome to tell you," she said. Kenny threw the instructions into his locker. Then he completely forgot about them. One week before it was due, he found them at the bottom of his locker under a wet glove.

"Mom! You gotta help me!" he said that night at home. He explained to her what had happened.

"Kenny," his dad said. "This is getting out of hand. You have to be more responsible." But then his dad helped him, the way he always did.

She sighed. "Okay, Kenny," she said. "I will help you this one last time. But this is it, really!"

She did some research online and helped create some charts and graphs while Kenny started writing. Sitting on his bed with his laptop, Kenny finally finished his report the night before it was due. He clicked "print" and got the report from the printer on his desk. Then he put the printout on the floor. He changed into his pajamas, throwing his clothes on the floor as well.

Think About It

- why do you think Kenny forgot about the science project?
- Do you know anybody like Kenny? What advice would you give him?

That morning, Kenny grabbed his poster that had the charts, graphs, and photos. But he couldn't

find his report, which was the most important part of the project. He remembered it was somewhere in his room and frantically moved stuff around trying to find it. Then he heard the bus coming down the street. His mom and dad had already left for work. If he missed the bus today, he'd have no one who could drive him. He grabbed his poster and ran out the door, catching the bus just in time.

Kenny thought his report turned out pretty well. After working so hard this past week, he was totally bummed about not having his report.

If he missed the bus today, he'd have no one who could drive him. He grabbed his poster and ran out the door, catching the bus just in time.

"I did it, but I just couldn't find it this morning. I'll promise to bring it tomorrow," Kenny pleaded with Mr. Jackson.

"I'm looking forward to seeing your report tomorrow, but it will be counted as late. I'm sorry, Kenny."

"You mean I still lose 25 points?"

"I'm afraid so, Kenny."

Think About It

- Where do you think Kenny should have placed his report? Do you have an area in your house where you always put your schoolwork?

- Why do you think Mr. Jackson took points off Kenny's project, even though Kenny said he did it and could turn it in the next day?

For guys like Kenny, being organized does not come naturally. Intelligence doesn't have anything to do with it. It's just a skill that needs to be learned. Being organized is especially important in middle school since it tends to be more hectic and demanding than elementary school.

If you train yourself to become organized, it will help you perform better in school. Decide on a plan to get yourself together, and make sure you are consistent with it. The more you follow a routine, the easier it is to stick with it.

To be organized, you don't have to change your personality. Just a few simple steps can really help. The first step, though, is recognizing the benefits of being prepared, then putting it at the top of your list of things to do. Doing a few small things every day can keep things neat so you can find them when you need them. While it may seem like a chore at first, it won't feel like that once things are basically where they are supposed to be. And you won't have the chore of rummaging through everything to find something underneath. If you need help establishing a plan, don't be afraid to ask an adult.

Work It Out

1. Use homework folders. Folders should be a different color for each class. After you do each assignment, put it in its correct folder *right away.*

2. Use a daily planner or online calendar to write down your assignments, and check it every day.

3. Have a spot at home where you always keep your backpack. And before you go to bed each night, make sure all your folders are in your backpack and ready to go.

The Last Word from Chris

If you are disorganized, get your act together before you lose something important. Here's a tip: Rather than waiting for the job to get really huge and wasting an entire Saturday on getting organized, break up the job. If your room is a mess, start by cleaning out a few dresser drawers. Then do your shoes. The next day do your computer stuff. It may take weeks. Then, just as importantly, keep things organized by putting stuff away as you use it. You'll never have to waste another Saturday again.

7

The Perfect Speech

Making a speech in front of the entire class is always a little stressful. You've seen it before—kids with trembling voices, maybe stuttering or speaking too quickly. Maybe you've seen shaking hands or knees. Maybe you've been one of those kids. A lot of guys are terrified of public speaking. They're afraid of messing up or looking stupid. Who wants to be embarrassed in front of all of his friends?

But you can't avoid giving presentations. Teachers assign them *because* they know kids are afraid of them. They want you to overcome your fear and learn an important life skill. So how do you deal with the stress of

public speaking? How do you stand calmly in front of a group of people and be relaxed? There has to be a secret you can learn, right? That is what Tyler wanted to know.

Tyler's Story

"Hey, Reggie, what's up?"

Tyler caught up to his friend and slapped him on the back.

"Oh, hey, Ty," Reggie grinned. The guys standing around his friend were all laughing.

"What's so funny?" Tyler asked.

"I was just telling everyone about my little encounter with Ms. Morton at our local drug store. . . . She was *not* happy to see me in line."

Reggie raised one eyebrow.

So how do you deal with the stress of public speaking? How do you stand calmly in front of a group of people and be relaxed?

"What was she buying?" Tyler asked, laughing in anticipation. Soon Tyler was laughing with the others while Reggie told his story.

That's just the way it was with Reggie. He was so funny. He loved getting people's attention—and he knew how to hold it. The amazing thing was that Reggie was the same way even during class presentations. He never seemed nervous!

Tyler was the complete opposite. Just thinking about public speaking made his mouth go dry. Whenever he had to do a class presentation, he worried he was going to say something wrong, or maybe even just forget completely what he was going to talk about. It was strange because, after all, neither of those things had actually ever happened to him. And Tyler wasn't what you'd call a shy kid. Somehow he just couldn't get over his fear of public speaking.

Think About It

- Are you afraid to talk to a large group? How have you dealt with that fear?

- Do you have a friend like Reggie who's not afraid of speaking in front of others?

- Do you think public speaking is an important skill? How could it be useful in your life?

Tyler had an oral book report to deliver in English on Wednesday, and he couldn't stop thinking about it. Monday night, he'd stayed up late rehearsing the presentation in his mind, even though he'd done the same thing on Sunday. He kept changing words, trying to find just the perfect ones.

Ms. Lake had said that when you give a speech, you shouldn't write out every word. You should make notes on index cards to remind you of what you want to say. That way, she said, you sound more natural. But Tyler couldn't help it. He had to write out everything.

Tuesday night he could barely sleep. When his turn came the next day, he walked to the front of the class with his heart pounding. Even though he'd practically memorized his report, he ended up reading the whole thing, barely looking up at all. He mumbled, too, and he read way too fast.

He wasn't surprised when he got a C on his presentation. Later in the week, Ms. Lake assigned class presentations to be delivered at the end of the term. Tyler wondered what he would have to do in order to avoid another C.

Think About It

- By putting pressure on himself to give a good oral report, was Tyler helping or hurting his chances to succeed?

- Tyler often went over his oral report in his mind. Is this a good way to practice? what methods do you think would be better?

Tyler realized he had a friend who could help him—Reggie! "You're so calm when you do your reports," he told his friend. "How do you do that? I'm already terrified about the history report." Tyler shook his head. "Can you help me out?"

"No problem," Reggie said. "The first thing you need to know is that you don't have to be perfect. People don't expect you to be perfect. You just have to know basically what you are talking about.

"I've messed up tons of times," Reggie continued, "said stupid stuff or forgot what I was going to say. It's no big deal. I always make a joke about it. That relaxes me, and it makes people laugh, too." Reggie paused for a minute. "You know, when I do that I think it actually makes my speech better. Everyone sees that I'm just like them."

Reggie explained that, instead of taking in the whole crowd, he would look only at three people—a person in the front row, a person in the middle of the room, and one in the back. "So I feel like I'm only talking to three people," Reggie said. "You talk to three people all the time . . . no big deal, right?"

Reggie also said that Tyler should practice his speech out loud. "That will help you get comfortable with what you're saying," he said, "and you'll get used to speaking up."

Think About It

- what do you think of Reggie's advice?
- Have you ever used any of these tips to give a presentation?

As Tyler prepared his oral report, he remembered what Reggie said. When it was time to speak in front of the class, Tyler felt a lot more confident as he stepped to the front of the room.

The first part of his report went smoothly. He used his index cards to remind him what to say;

he didn't read them word for word. But then, when he flipped the third index card aside, he realized card number four was missing!

"I . . . I . . ." he stuttered. He stopped cold and started to panic.

Then he remembered how Reggie said it was okay to mess up—he just had to keep going. "Sorry everyone, but index card number four seems to have run away. It must not have liked my report."

A couple people in the class giggled. Tyler's teacher smiled a little. "Can you continue, Tyler?" she asked.

"Uh, sure, I think so," replied Tyler. He gave the outline of what he remembered from card four, and then he was safely back to his notes. The rest of the report went well. He even made a few more jokes and got some more laughs. And Ms. Lake seemed pleased with his work. Tyler knew he wouldn't have to be afraid of speaking in public again.

"I . . . I . . ." he stuttered. He stopped cold and started to panic.

Think About It

- why do you think Reggie told Tyler to joke about messing something up during his oral report?

- when you give a speech or an oral report, do you follow Reggie's advice and look at just a few people? Do you use any other tricks to help you give a better presentation?

- How does practicing a speech out loud help?

Many people have a fear of speaking in front of a large group. The most common reason for this is that they are afraid of looking foolish in front of everyone. But remember that the people in the audience *want* you to succeed. Think about the times when you've been in an audience. Aren't you rooting for the speaker?

If you're nervous to speak, take a few deep breaths first. This slows down your heartbeat and helps you feel more relaxed. When you relax, you'll think more clearly and probably won't talk as fast. And Reggie was right. One of the best ways to overcome a fear of public speaking is to say to yourself, "So what?" So what if you make a mistake? What do you do when you make a mistake among friends? You smile and correct yourself. The people in your audience are just people. You can smile and correct yourself in front of them, too. It's a tried and true rule among public speakers—even the president does it!

As with other fears, the more you face your fear of public speaking, the less power it will have over you. That's probably a main reason why your teachers assign oral reports in the first place. They are giving you practice for an important skill that will serve you for the rest of your life.

Work It Out

1. Don't be afraid to rely just on notes. If you get stuck, you can refresh your memory. But you won't be reading, so you can still make eye contact and sound natural.

2. Practice your speech out loud. Do it for your parents, friends, your little sister, your dog—even in front of the mirror.

3. Take a deep breath and smile at your audience. Concentrate on standing up straight and not speaking too quickly.

4. Look for opportunities to practice public speaking, such as student council or debate.

Last Word from Chris

You want to know an easy way to be a good public speaker? Don't consider yourself a public speaker! When we give a speech, we think we have to do as well as the president. We think we have to be perfect and not forget anything. Don't try to be like someone else. Instead, just be who you are. If you use humor when you talk, then do that when you give a speech. Your audience is expecting to hear *you* speak, not the president.

8

The Project Leader

Everyone has to do group projects. Teachers assign group projects at every grade from elementary school through college. In fact, depending on their jobs, many adults have to do group projects, too. Being able to work effectively in groups is a very important skill that you are likely to need throughout your life.

Teachers assign group projects for lots of reasons. Sometimes it makes doing a project more fun. Other times, a teacher wants to see how well students work with others, especially if they don't often work together in the classroom.

However, group projects can also be frustrating. The members of the group

may not get along well or one member may not do a
fair share of the work. See what happens to Ray when
he is assigned to do a group project.

Ray's Story

Ray generally liked doing
group work. Usually it
was more creative than
regular school work. He
liked designing posters

Group projects can also be
frustrating. The members of
the group may not get along
well or one member may not
do a fair share of the work.

and making videos for projects. Whenever they got to
choose their own groups, Ray and his friends always
worked together. They could trust each other to
finish their own parts of the project. They always had
a great time, and they usually got good grades, too.

The only problem was history. Mr. Stephens never let the students choose their own groups. Ray had been lucky—during the first two projects of the year, he'd been put in groups with friends both times. But this time, when Mr. Stephens made the groups for the Civil War project, Ray groaned. Miguel and Zack were all right. But Dean! *Dean's such a slacker,* Ray thought. *I don't want to get a bad grade because of stupid Dean!*

Think About It

- why did Ray usually enjoy doing group projects?

- when the teacher assigned who was going to work on each project, why was Ray upset?

- Have you ever had to work on a group project with people you didn't like? How did you handle it?

When the group met to discuss who was going to do what, Ray took over the conversation.

"Okay, so, we have to do a presentation on the Battle of Gettysburg. Miguel, you talk about weapons and fighting. Zack, you research the generals."

Miguel and Zack high-fived. "All right!" exclaimed Miguel. "The military stuff is sweet!"

"I'll take the hard part," continued Ray. "I'll talk about how the battle affected the rest of the war.

Dean, you can do the Gettysburg Address—that will be the easiest part."

Dean looked a little resentful, but he didn't say anything.

"Okay, good," finished Ray. "Let's work on our parts and get together in three days. Then we can start writing our speeches and getting props next week."

When the group got together again in three days, Ray, Miguel, and Zack all had their research done. Dean came with a mostly blank piece of paper. All he had done was scribble his name and jot down a couple of thoughts.

"Sorry, guys," Dean said, not sounding sorry at all. "I guess I forgot. You seem to have everything under control without me, though."

Think About It

- Why was Ray so worried about having Dean on his project team?
- Have you ever been part of a project where one person told everyone else what to do? How did you react?

Ray was fuming. *If Dean thinks he can get away with this . . .* Ray thought. He kept his temper in check, however. Gritting his teeth, Ray replied, "That's okay, Dean. We'll help you catch up."

Ray decided the group's assignments for the next couple of days. When they met again the next time, Dean still hadn't done his share.

This time, Ray was sick of doing Dean's work. "What is your problem, Dean? It's gonna be your fault if we get a bad grade."

"Who died and made you boss?" Dean said sarcastically. "If everything's gotta be your way, then do the work yourself."

Dean smirked and walked away. Ray was ticked off, but who was he kidding? Dean could get away

with it because he knew Ray wouldn't let the team get a bad grade.

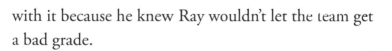

Think About It

- When Dean didn't do his fair share of the work at the start of the project, should Ray have talked to him then? Why?

- What was the reason Dean gave for not doing his work?

- What are some things Ray could have done differently when the group first got together?

- If you were Ray, would you do Dean's work? At this point, is there anything else Ray could do?

Every good student's worst nightmare is being stuck with a slacker in a group project. You and the other members are doing what you're supposed to while one member does nothing. How do you fix a problem like that?

First, you have to confront this person and find out if there is a real problem. Ask with respect rather than being accusatory. Maybe he is having difficulties at home or has a few other projects he is working on at the same time. If there is a good reason for him not doing his fair share of the work, try to be understanding. Try to come up with a fair solution, like taking one part of his task away and dividing it up among the rest of the group. But be clear that he has to come through with the rest of the project.

However, sometimes a person just refuses to do his share of the work, or promises to help but never follows through. This can be a serious problem. If you are unable to solve the problem on your own, then it may be wise to get the teacher involved, especially if everyone on the project is receiving the same grade.

Work It Out

1. Give people a chance. Having low expectations of a group member does not help. If you and the rest of the group provide a positive example, he may learn from you and improve his effort.

2. Make sure everyone has a say in who does what in a group project. Try to promote teamwork.

3. When you see someone not doing his part of the project, don't ignore the problem. That will only make things worse. When you talk to him, be firm but not angry. Work with him to adjust his assignments.

The Last Word from Chris

Sometimes there are good ways to deal with a group slacker: helping him feel included in making decisions, making sure he can handle his assignments, and talking to the teacher if he's just dead weight. Sometimes, though, you've got to make the best of a bad situation and take on the extra work. It's not fair, but, like you've heard a million times, life isn't always fair. Sometimes you just have to roll up your sleeves and get stuff done yourself.

9

The Workaholic

"Y ou need to go to college to get a good job." Adults are always saying that, and it's true for many guys. But the situation is not that simple. Attending a four-year university is expensive. Even if you graduate at the top of your class, there's no guarantee you'll be able to afford to go to the school you want.

That fact can lead to stress for many guys. Even if they're not old enough to work a "real" job, they still feel the pressure to start earning money and saving for college. Pretty soon, their afternoons and weekends are booked with mowing lawns or delivering papers. And that leaves no time for being a

Pete was a guy like that. He became so worried about his future, he forgot to live in the present.

Pete's Story

"We are so very proud of you, Petey."

Pete rolled his eyes. His parents were always saying that. It embarrassed him, but he had to smile a little, too. Those words meant a lot coming from them. His parents were both second-generation immigrants—their parents had immigrated to the United States in the 1960s. Pete's father still ran Nick's Deli, the store his father had founded in 1971.

> Even if you graduate at the top of your class, there's no guarantee you'll be able to afford to go to the school you want.

To Pete, it felt like Nick's Deli was the setting for almost all of his childhood memories. That's where he lost his first tooth; he learned to read at one of the faded yellow tables. His parents were always there, working, and so that's where he grew up.

"We never got to go to college, Pete," his mother once told him. "But maybe, if we save enough, you'll be able to." And, more than anything, Pete wanted the honor of becoming the first person in his family to earn a college degree.

Pete was years away from even applying to college, but his head was bursting with ideas about how he was going to pay for it.

Think About It

- why was it so important for Pete to go to college?

- was Pete worrying about the cost of college too soon? why do you believe that?

- what would you do if you wanted to go to college but couldn't afford it?

"Why don't you do stuff around the neighborhood to earn money? You could mow people's lawns, maybe." Pete's mom leaned against her broom for a minute as she talked to him. She'd already said "no way" to having him work at the store until he was old enough to be a legal employee.

"Pete P's Lawn and Garden Service," Pete said slowly. He liked the sound of it. As soon as he went home, he designed a flyer for his business. For the next week, he went around the neighborhood knocking on doors and passing out his ad. Soon he had a list of neighbors who were happy to pay him to mow their lawns and pull up their dandelions.

Pete had to go out and actually buy one of those daily calendars adults use because his schedule got so busy. He had appointments every day after school and during the weekends until dark. Sometimes it was stressful trying to finish quickly to make it to his next client on time, but the money was rolling in.

Pete knew exactly what to do. With his parents' help, he invested the money in a special college fund. The deal with his college fund was that the more money he put in and the *earlier* he did it, the more interest it would pile up. And, as he understood it, interest was like free extra money.

Whenever Pete didn't want to get out of bed early on a Saturday or couldn't bear the thought of dragging his tired body to another person's yard, he remembered his college fund.

Think About It

• Do you think Pete working so soon to save money is the right thing to do?

• What are some of the possible consequences of Pete working nearly every day?

Pete's phone wouldn't stop vibrating.

"Okay, okay," he said. He turned off the lawn mower and pulled out his phone.

It was a text from Malcolm: "Beach on Sat.?"

Good old Malcolm. Most of Pete's other friends had stopped inviting him to stuff—the parties on Friday nights, ballgames, or afternoons at the mall. Pete pretended he didn't care. It *was* easier not having to hear about all the fun his friends were having while he had to work. But still . . . Pete smiled when he got the text.

"Sorry dude," he texted back.

After a second, his phone buzzed. "Stop working so much! U r missing out on life!!!"

Pete yanked hard on the lawn mower cord, and the machine roared into action. *Easy for you to say*, he thought as he pushed the mower through the thick grass. Beads of sweat ran down his face.

Malcolm is so spoiled, Pete thought as he wiped his sleeve across his mouth. Malcolm's father was

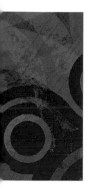

president of some company downtown. In fact, none of Pete's friends could understand what he was going through. Either they had money or they just didn't care about college the way he did. He couldn't help it if they didn't understand.

Think About It

- Is it mean of Pete's friends to stop inviting him to stuff?

- why does Pete think his friends can't understand his situation?

That Saturday, Pete got sick—throwing up, feverish sick.

"I'm calling the neighbors to cancel for you," his mother announced. She was right. There was no way he could mow lawns today.

One thing Pete hated about being sick was being alone. His parents were at the store, and his little sister was out with friends as usual. He could watch only so many game shows before the television gave him a headache. As Pete stared at the ceiling, uncomfortable thoughts started creeping in. He thought of Malcolm's message: "You're missing out on life." Why had it made him so mad?

He thought of Malcolm's message: "You're missing out on life." Why had it made him so mad?

Pete remembered that his friends were at the beach right now. In his mind, he saw them playing volleyball, drinking cold soda, and soaking up the sun. He could hear the seagulls and smell the water.

Pete felt like his heart was being squeezed. His eyes felt hot. He smacked his fist down on his bed. "I hate my life," he whispered. He resolved right then and there to change it—if he could just figure out how to begin.

Think About It

- What advice would you give to Pete?

- Have you ever been in a situation where you felt like you had to live up to your parents' unspoken expectations?

- Have you ever felt stuck in a situation the same way Pete feels stuck?

Planning for the future is a wise thing to do, but it can't be the only thing you do. Pete was working so much, he was starting to lose his friends and miss out on experiencing the fun things in life. He was working to save money for college, and while that is a worthy goal, it can't be the only way he spends his time.

As you could tell, Pete was starting to resent his life and having to spend so much time working. Pete felt pressure from his parents, even though they never actually asked him to save for college. Work just became a means to an end. When work is only about money, it's easy to start to dislike it.

You may even start to resent the fact that you have to work so hard to achieve your goal. As you look at what you are missing out on, the idea of attending college may not be as appealing as you once thought. You might ask yourself: "Is this really worth it?" That's why it's important to strike a balance between planning for the future, working to attain your goals, and living in the present. Having a good social life can also be important to your future success.

Work It Out

1. Before deciding to work in order to pay for college, learn about scholarships and grants available to people in your situation. When the time comes, apply for as many of them as possible to help pay for college.

2. As part of your schedule, make sure you leave some free time available for yourself. Use that time to then hang out with friends or to do something fun.

The Last Word from Chris

"Nothing in excess." The ancient Greek thinker Solon is said to have first spoken those famous words. If you think about it, Pete's motives were totally right. He was doing everything he was supposed to—he just got carried away. Everybody has an area in their life where they go overboard. Maybe for you it's watching too much television, eating too much, or even working out too much. I can't think of a single thing that *isn't* bad for you when it's taken to an extreme—can you? Fortunately, Pete noticed the bad feeling we all get when we lose control. He paid attention to his gut and admitted he was wrong. He's going to be okay.

Navigating school might seem as impossible as fitting a square peg through a round hole. So many different things are thrown at you at the same time that it is easy to feel overwhelmed. You have to deal with social issues, like what to wear and how to act and why someone who used to talk to you no longer does. At the same time, you have to overcome new fears like taking difficult standardized tests or speaking in front of the whole class.

What you have to remember is you are not alone. Everyone in your school is facing the same problems you are, whether they want to admit it or not. The "cool" people are worrying about whether they are still cool or not. The guy who is making really good grades is worried about having to one day pay for college.

When dealing with stuff like this, the answers won't always come easily. In fact, you may not be able to come up with a solution to a problem at all, and that's fine. At that point, ask for help. A parent, a teacher, or a friend would be more than happy to give you support and help. Don't get so caught up in the everyday drama around you that you forget you have a support system. And no matter what you think, your current problem will likely seem less stressful with time. Take time to relax and enjoy the present.

Don't stress!

Chris

Remember, a healthful life is about balance. Now that you know how to walk that path, pay it forward to a friend or even yourself! Remember the Work It Out tips throughout this book, and then take these steps to get healthy and get going.

- When dealing with your education and future career, remember to always have balance in your life.

- Trying to change who you are to become part of the cool crowd could backfire on you. Change can be good, but don't forget who you are.

- Figure out which after-school activities are more important than others. That way, if you start to feel overwhelmed, you will know which activities you wouldn't mind cutting out.

- If you have dyslexia or another type of learning disability, remember you are not alone. You can overcome challenges with time, help, and good strategies.

- If someone is trying to steer you toward a career that you may not want, then speak up! You are the only person who really knows what may or may not interest you.

- If you feel yourself start to get overanxious before or during a test, try to relax. Take a deep breath and clear your mind of any negative thoughts. By believing you will do well, you often experience success.

- Try to remain organized. Sticking to a routine will make doing your schoolwork—and living your life—easier.

- When preparing for a report or speech, practice often and practice out loud. Then you won't be as nervous when you have to do it in front of people.

- When you are doing a group project, don't start by dictating what each person should do. Decide on who is going to do what as a group. That way everyone will agree with the plan.

- Wanting to start working in order to save money is great. But don't let your goal become an obsession. So make sure you schedule some fun into your life.

Additional Resources

Selected Bibliography

Dawson, Peg, and Richard Guare. *Smart but Scattered.* New York: The Guilford Press, 2009.

Giacobello, John. *Everything You Need to Know About the Dangers of Overachieving: A Guide for Relieving Pressure and Anxiety.* New York: The Rosen Publishing Group, Inc., 2000.

Kutner, Lawrence. *Making Sense of Your Teenager.* New York: William Morrow and Company, Inc., 1997.

Marshall, Abigail. *The Everything Parent's Guide to Children with Dyslexia.* Avon, MA: Adams Media, 2004.

Further Reading

Kutscher, Martin, and Marcella Moran. *Organizing the Disorganized Child: Simple Strategies to Succeed in School.* New York: Harper Studio, 2009.

Shaywitz, Sally. *Overcoming Dyslexia: A New and Complete Science-based Program for Reading Problems at Any Level.* New York: Alfred A. Knopf, 2003.

Web Sites

To learn more about managing school and career paths, visit ABDO Publishing Company online at **www.abdopublishing.com**. Web sites about managing school and career paths are featured on our Book Links page. These links are routinely monitored and updated to provide the most current information available.

For More Information

For more information on this subject, contact or visit the following organizations:

Boys and Girls Club of America
1-800-854-CLUB
www.bgca.org
The Boys and Girls Club of America has local clubs in communities across the country. Clubs provide a safe place for children to learn and form relationships after school.

Learning Disabilities Association of America
4156 Library Road, Pittsburgh, PA, 15234
412-341-1515
www.ldanatl.org
This organization provides advice and resources for people with learning disabilities and the people who help them.

Glossary

adolescent
> A child at the stage of life ranging from puberty to the end of high school.

anxiety
> An overwhelming sense of fear often marked by sweating, tension, and increased pulse.

aptitude
> A strong ability.

aptitude test
> A standardized test that measures a person's skills.

dyslexia
> A learning disability that causes difficulty in reading.

exclusive
> Limited to few people.

Individualized Education Plan
> A document for students with special needs that sets a student's personal goals for the year and outlines what resources the school will provide to support those goals.

masculine

Relating to men.

sexism

Discrimination based on a person's sex.

stereotype

An advance judgment of someone based on a group or category he or she belongs to.

Index

About the Author

J Chris Roselius has been an award-winning writer and journalist for more than 15 years. A graduate of the University of Texas, he has written numerous books. Currently residing in Houston, Texas, he enjoys spending time with his wife and two children. When not attending baseball games with them, he likes to watch a variety of college and professional sports. He also enjoys traveling, watching history and science programs, and reading the newspaper in order to keep up with current events.

Photo Credits